amicus illustrated

# MATH WORLD
# COUNTING
# CHANGE

BY BRIDGET HEOS ILLUSTRATED BY KATYA LONGHI

Amicus Illustrated is published by Amicus
P.O. Box 1329, Mankato, MN 56002
www.amicuspublishing.us

Editor: Rebecca Glaser
Designer: Kathleen Petelinsek

Library of Congress Cataloging-in-Publication Data
Heos, Bridget, author.
 Counting change / By Bridget Heos ; illustrated by Katya Longhi.
    pages cm. — (Math world)
 Summary: "Aiden helps his little brother Mason make change at a
yard sale so that he can buy a new video game, which they will
then share"— Provided by publisher.
 Audience: Grade K to 3.
 Includes bibliographical references.
 ISBN 978-1-60753-462-4 (library binding) —
 ISBN 978-1-60753-677-2 (ebook)
 1. Counting—Juvenile literature. 2. Coins, American—Juvenile
literature. 3. Money—Juvenile literature. I. Longhi, Katya, illustrator.
II. Title.
 QA113.H457 2015
 513.2'11—dc23                                        2013032470

Printed in the United States of America at Corporate Graphics
in North Mankato, Minnesota.

10 9 8 7 6 5 4 3 2 1

## ABOUT THE AUTHOR

Bridget Heos is the author of more than
60 books for kids and teens, including many
books for Amicus Illustrated and her recent
picture book *Mustache Baby* (Houghton
Mifflin Harcourt, 2013). She lives in Kansas City
with her husband and four children. Visit her
on the Web at www.authorbridgetheos.com.

## ABOUT THE ILLUSTRATOR

Katya Longhi was born in southern Italy. She
studied illustration at the Nemo NT Academy
of Digital Arts in Florence. She loves to create
dream worlds in her illustrations. She currently
lives in northern Italy with her Prince Charming.

"What's all this, Mason?"

"Oh, hey, Aiden. I'm selling stuff so I can buy Donut Derby 12000."

"I love that game!"

"Yeah, but it costs $30. And nobody brought enough money to buy anything."

"I'm sorry. That book costs one dollar. You only have four quarters. You don't have enough money, either!"

"Um, Mason, four quarters
equals one dollar."
"Really?"

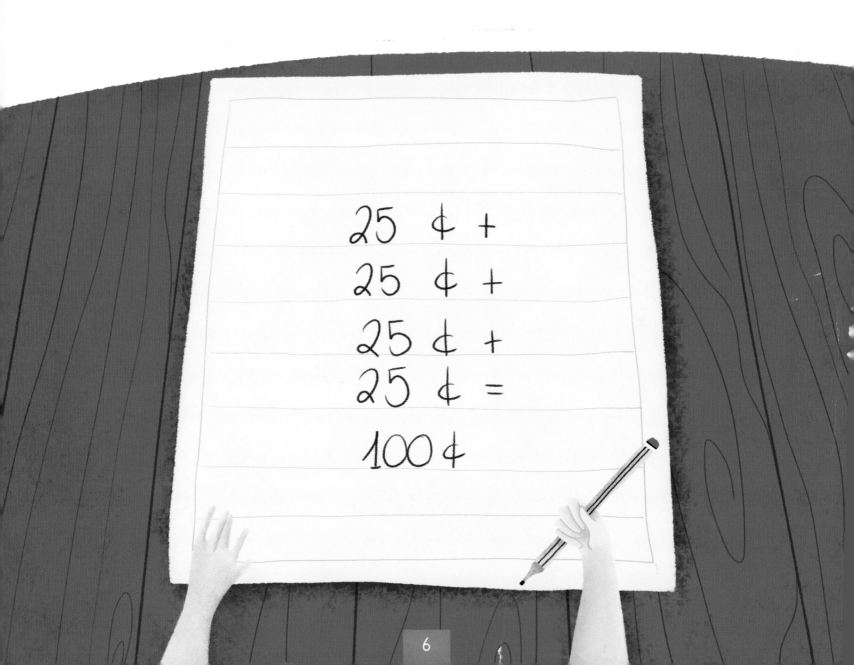

. . . and 100 cents equals one dollar. I'll help you make change today . . . if you let me play Donut Derby 12000."

"Deal!" Mason says with a smile.

"You need one dollar bill or four quarters, not 10 dimes."

"Ten dimes also equals a dollar, Mason. Watch."

"Oh, I see! I guess you do have enough!"
Mason says. "Wait, where did she go?"

"Mason, before you scare away another customer, how many nickels are in one dollar?"

"A trillion? A gazillion? Infinity?"

"No, a nickel is worth five cents. Count by fives until you get to 100.

"So 20 nickels make a dollar. And how many did he give you?"

"Twenty. Right! Thanks, Matt," Mason says.

"Why is a nickel bigger than a dime, Aiden? A dime should be bigger. It's worth more."

"You just have to remember that a dime is smaller but worth more."

1¢ +
1¢ +
1¢ +
1¢ +
1¢ +
1¢ =
$2

"Well, Mason, do you think 200 cents equals two dollars?"

"Yes! And I'll show you why."

"Thank you," Aiden says.

"See Mason, you can combine different coins.

Two dimes and a nickel are the same as a quarter."

$$10¢ + 10¢ + 5¢ = 25¢$$

"You have too much money. Choose something more expensive," Mason says.

"Mason, you can give her change. Start at 50 cents and count up to one dollar. For quarters, count by 25. Starting at 50, count 75, then 100. She gets two quarters back.

"Here you go, 50 cents is your change," Mason says.

"I think I get this. Amy's item is $2.50. But she gave me $3.00, so I count up $2.75, $3.00. She gets two quarters back. Right, Aiden?"

"Right, Mason! To make 50 cents, you can also give her 10 nickels, 50 pennies, or a combination of coins."

"So coins add up to make cents and dollars. And if a customer has too much money, coins can also add up to make change."

"Awesome."

"How much is this remote control helicopter?" a new customer asks.

"Ten dollars," Mason says.

"Great! I have 1,000 pennies," the customer says.

"That's a lot of counting, but those pennies add up, Mason. You have $16.25. We're more than halfway to buying Donut Derby!"

# GLOSSARY

**cent** The smallest amount of money. 100 cents equal 1 dollar.

**change** The difference, in dollars and cents, between what is paid and what is owed.

**coins** Money made of metal.

**dime** A coin that equals 10 cents.

**dollar** An amount that equals 100 cents.

**equals** Is the same amount as.

**nickel** A coin that equals 5 cents.

**penny** A coin that equals 1 cent.

**quarter** A coin that equals 25 cents.

# READ MORE

Burstein, John. Dollars and Sense: Developing Good Money Habits. Slim Goodbody's Life Skills 101. New York: Crabtree Pub., 2011.

Cleary, Brian P. A Dollar, a Penny, How Much and How Many? Math is Categorial. Minneapolis: Millbrook Press, 2012.

Loughran, Donna. Carnival Coins: How Will We Count Our Money? Chicago: Norwood House Press, 2013.

Penn, M. W. Counting Money! Pebble Math. North Mankato, Minn.: Capstone Press, 2012.

# WEBSITES

ABCya! Learn to Count Money
http://www.abcya.com/counting_money.htm
Practice counting coins and bills in this game. Choose your level and challenge yourself.

H.I.P. Pocket Change Website
http://www.usmint.gov/kids/
Learn about how coins are made, the designs on coins, and how to collect coins from the U.S. Mint.

It's My Life. Money. PBSKids Go!
http://pbskids.org/itsmylife/money/index.html
Get ideas about how to earn money, save money, and spend it wisely.

*Every effort has been made to ensure that these websites are appropriate for children. However, because of the nature of the Internet, it is impossible to guarantee that these sites will remain active indefinitely or that their contents will not be altered.*